Table of CONTENTS

©Copyright 2015 by Gordon R Kaesemeyer

Prologue

A special thanks to my dear friend **Bubba** for keeping this manuscript safe for "No More Rip' Offs" for more than twenty years. The following information remains as relevant today as the day I dictated this to Bubba. This information was my departing gesture for the many thousands of customers and friends I left behind when they asked, "Who is going to fix my car now?"

I closed a chapter in my life in southern California in 1995. I was the owner-operator of a very successful and honest auto repair business known as "THE SHOP"

I have witnessed many questionable procedures during my many years in the auto repair business. I came to the understanding that most car manufacturers have designed their cars to fail. After the warranty is gone, you the consumer will just buy a new maintenance-free car. No repair required! Whatever happened to changing gear oil, brake fluid and coolant? Over time I noticed engine oil was missing zinc which was used for extra lubrication in older engines to mitigate the wear and tear of the camshaft.

Newer engine use roller lifters or overhead camshafts using "cam followers/rockers," so zinc isn't necessary. We could have been warned. Back in 2005, I had a rash of old engines have failures of the camshafts so I started asking around to see if other shops had also noticed. I discovered everyone had! It was then I began researching to find out exactly what was changed.

I found out the manufacturers were claiming it caused damage to the federally required catalytic converter and it wasn't needed for newer cars. They sell a zinc additive now for use in older cars. Diesel grade oils still contain zinc. Castrol 30 wt. oil still has it, and is good oil for those old, loosely built engines.

Technical information on new cars is often not available to the public until after the warranty expires, however the Internet is changing this practice. Information is being made public via internet platforms such as *Youtube,* chat rooms, and blog sites by vehicle owners and enthusiasts. There is now a trend of relevant and current information at the consumers fingertips thus surpassing the manufacturers hold on the technical information. Anyone nowadays can get their "Gear Head" via *Youtube.*

Historically, technicians at the dealer level have specific areas of training and expertise, resulting in a smaller understanding of the complete vehicle thus keeping it even more proprietary. Some mechanics have opened corner garages taking advantage of the need for car repairs at a more affordable price. A mechanic is someone with a few tools and a little bit of success in fixing car by replacing parts. He is often solving the problems at the expense of the undereducated vehicle owner. He may be guessing at the problem by using a "replace the Black Box" approach. How many times have you been called back with a quote for additional parts and labor required? Perhaps the first parts didn't fix your problem like you were told?

With the help of this book you, the consumer, will learn to develop a strategy to navigate the auto repair gauntlet without feeling you were taken advantage of by *"Joe the Mechanic."*

My love for automobiles has been a central focus for my entire career. I read every motor manual I could get my hands on starting in Fifth grade. A quote from Henry Ford made me realize the importance I could play in the game by being knowledgeable about cars; "If I could guarantee the cars would come back to me for repairs I would give them the car!"

I ask an engineer one time what the worst part of being in his profession was? He said being sent back to the drawing board to design it to "FAIL" in two years.

People say to be a doctor one must read a book every week for four years, or a book a month for their entire life, as per Brian Tracy, the author of *"Million Dollar Habits."*

If that is the case I am definitely the "Car Doctor."

Gordon Kaesemeyer

Introduction

Most of you have been ripped off by an auto mechanic at one time or another whether you knew it or not. Maybe you realized it the next day when your car's problem still was there? My thirty-five years in the trade has taught me one thing: You, the consumer, do not understand how to choose a decent auto mechanic, or protect yourself from being oversold or handle any misunderstandings as they occur.

I will explain over the next several pages the possible potential recourses you can use with a little perseverance, **this book will insure you will never be** *ripped off again!*

The automobile repair **rip off** has been refined to an art form. Your car is not the first car needing a specific repair and somebody somewhere has figured out how to fix that same problem. It is not a miracle or a new concept. Somebody has seen this problem before and it has probably had a technical bulletin written about it. Every model has its inherent problems, because they are produced on an assembly line.

Consider the automotive industries' frequent recalls to replace this item or that. You will only hear about those involving safety concerns or law suits, but there are hundreds a month across the automotive industry.

First, communication is critical in the diagnosis of your car's problem. Imitation, charades and making whirling, grinding, skipping, bumping sounds probably won't get you the results you are looking for. All car problems, even if they seem intermittent, can be duplicated. The trick is to make note of when and what makes your car behave abnormally.

I had a customer describe a buzzing noise when his car shifted into second gear. The dealer had replaced his car's entire drive train.

No-one had ever gone for a ride with the car's owner. It turned out he could only make the noise happen on the hill near his home. When I went with him to the location where the noise occurred, I heard the noise, I asked him to stop the car. I then took off his front license plate frame and the noise went away.

The customer was so pleased he sent me a bottle of scotch every Christmas for years.

Everybody wins when mechanics take the time to understand the customer's automotive problem and that is was why I was so successful! I also didn't let their problem become my problem. That costs extra!

Once you can make your car "act up" you are ready to recreate the circumstances for the technician. A verbal description of the problem pales compared to an actual test drive with *"Joe Mechanic"* sitting beside you. So hit the road if it's not obvious. Learn how to duplicate that intermittent problem

Choosing A Facility

Now you are ready to find a repair facility which will meet your needs. Your options are complex, yet can be simplified by following a few guidelines. The choices are dealerships such as *Ford, Chrysler, General Motors, Toyota, Honda, Nissan,* or franchises and chains like *PEP Boys, Sears, AAmco Transmissions, Firestone, Econo Lube & Tune*, or independents like *"Joe's Garage"* or specialty shops that repair only mufflers, carburetors, radiators, or perform simple tune ups.

ToonClips.com   #4123   service@toonclips.com

When traveling, take your car to a national chain facility because all repairs contain some form of warranty. This allows the completed repair, to be disputed and /or honored at any one of the nationwide chain store locations. Now is a good time to already have **AAA** *Membership* because benefits are enormous,

Membership includes twenty-four towing and roadside assistance, and/or referrals to one of their approved repair facilities.

Another alternative is to call a nearby parts supplier such as *"Napa Auto Parts"* because they will have certified garages in the local area.

I owned two such facilities for a total of twenty years and was approved by both AAA and Napa Auto Parts.

I recommend calling **1-800-LET-NAPA** to be referred to an affiliated garage. Repairs performed through either of these centers come with a twelve month or twelve-thousand mile parts and labor warranty which is honored nationwide.

Consider looking on www.yelp.com to see what other customers are posting about the garages and their ability to fix cars and the quality of the customer service.

"Bob thinks it's your distributor and I think it's definitely the spark plugs, so we are going to compromise and replace your water pump."

The Initial Phone Call

After identifying your car's specific problem, consider the level of
competence of the technician to whom you are speaking. Here is
a list of potential questions.

- What is your hourly labor rate?

- Is there a minimum diagnostic charge? If so, how much is it?

- Have you seen this same problem before? How many cars have you successfully repaired with this exact problem? If you are familiar with my car's problem, will you require a full diagnostic time? Many times the mechanic will have a good idea of what your problem is by your description of it, yet will still want to charge a diagnostic fee. The Industry standard is one hour for this. Remember, everything is negotiable. If he is charging you a diagnostic fee but is also telling you he's pretty sure he knows what the problem is then what else is he going to charge you, simply because he can?

- How long does this type of job usually take to repair? Everyone uses a labor guide these days. They are fair and accurate measures of time required performing the task.

- Equally important to the answers of your questions is the mechanic's attitude while answering them. Anything less than a concerned response may cost you more money in the long run. If the mechanic is not interested in answering your questions to your satisfaction, then you may need to keep looking for another mechanic.

The Drive By

Before blindly taking your car in for service, I recommend driving by the shop for a visual inspection of the facility. Are the mechanics busy? Just like decent restaurants, the good ones are busy.

Is the shop clean? This will be a reflection on the shop's ability to keep your vehicle clean. Is there real work being done or are the mechanics visiting with each other?

After parking your car, walk by the actual repair area. Try to get someone's attention and after briefly identifying your problem area, ask who, in their opinion, would by the best qualified mechanic to do the job. This allows you to ask for a mechanic by name that has a reputation of fixing car problems like yours.

Case in point: I worked in a shop heavily advertised as *"General Motors Specialists,"* and I was a factory trained

GM Technician who was very specific and intensely thorough in my work.

After my first day at work I realized that the owners and lead mechanics had extremely limited knowledge of General Motor automobiles! I asked them why they advertised as GM Specialists when it was apparent they had such a minor degree of product knowledge. I have never forgotten their answer. "We had to declare a specialty to secure our lease in this automotive repair complex, and Ford was already taken."

The boss then went on to explain how their earlier customers had literally paid hundreds of dollars for them to learn how to fix "General Motors" cars. "Diagnosis" is performing inspections and performing specific tests to confirm a defective part or connection is bad.

The industry has created simple "black box" changers and we refer to them as "mechanics."   Actual trained technicians are few and far between. There are many ways to get training. Schools cost money. Don't be a school.

The Service Order

There is an important distinction between explaining the car's problem and showing or demonstrating it. Don't tell them what the problem is. Let them tell you. If you tell the service writer, "I need a tune up" because your car is running poorly, you will get a tune up and most likely still have the same problem. Let mechanics do their jobs.

You have already found out who the best technician is for your car's problem by asking those that know. The technicians know amongst themselves who is best. Now ask if the mechanic will accompany you on a test drive so you can demonstrate your problem. No matter how obvious it may seem to you, a mechanic may not know which problem you are referring to. You of course are referring to the new one not the other

3 noises that have been ongoing and you thought was normal.

According to the Bureau of Auto Repair, it is your legal right to ask for the old parts back, but you need to do it when service order is written and make sure it is noted on the order. If you get an old part back you can assume you probably got a new one even if you don't know what you are looking at. This practice keeps honest mechanics honest.

Now it is time to walk around the car with the mechanic and make note as to whether they document any vehicle damage. Do not leave anything of value in the car and make sure you have at least a half a tank of fuel when you take it in. It can get pretty expensive to pay a shop to put fuel in for your car so they can repair, then test drives your car.

THE ESTIMATE

Once the technician has experienced the car's problem as demonstrated by you, they will write up a service agreement concerning needed repairs. This written document needs to clearly state the problem and the name of the technician who experienced it with you.

All written estimates must contain the vehicle and customer information, date, time, estimated amount to diagnose or repair and, most importantly, your signature authorizing the described work to be accomplished. Be sure to keep a copy of this estimate as this can be valuable protection from any future misunderstandings of what was expected and agreed upon. Be sure to inspect your vehicle before leaving and after picking up your repaired vehicle for any damage that happened while in the mechanic's possession. Accidents happen and anything of consequence must be dealt with at this time to be validated.

No fair bringing up a scratch or dent a week later. Also take a look at the tops of your car's fenders, as they may not have been covered while the mechanic was working. At a minimum they should be wiped down and you need to insure your vehicle paint is in the same condition as when you turned it over to them.

You can call a parts store yourself and inquire about the cost of the part **before authorizing repair!** The part will cost you a little bit more to buy it from an installer. Twenty percent is an acceptable markup to pay. Any more than that, you need to ask ... Why? Everything is negotiable. Sometimes mechanics will gouge you on the part but not on the labor. Case in point: I recently got a call.

A lady asking me about a noise that she heard in her *Subaru.* It turned out to be the left rear wheel bearing. The mechanic told her the bearing was seven-hundred-and-fifty dollars. I told her to price the bearing and then take the car elsewhere to have it repaired. Also, when you are getting the estimate ask the mechanics to confirm the previous diagnosis before repairing it. The lady was able to get her car repaired for half the price she was originally quoted.

This is what caused me to add this particular information to "No More Rip Offs'. After you get a quote from the repair facility, check out the validity of the price quote <u>before</u> authorizing any repairs.   Call a couple of shops, randomly, and ask how much they would charge for the exact same repair. Call a parts store. Check the parts price. You might want to take your car elsewhere. You might just find someone you can trust!

"You just Got Ripped Off"?

There is little that can be done when you discover you've been ripped off but a place to start is the *Bureau of Auto Repair* (if you reside in California), the *Consumer Protection Agency*, or small claims court.

Every county has a fraud division with the district attorney's office so don't be afraid to use it.

All of these options will require more of your time and may cost you even more money to find justice and stop the rip off. The question you need to ask is, how much justice can you afford? Consider this option; **pay with a credit card!**

Allow me to explain.

Credit Cards are the safest way to purchase *anything.* You are protected against fraud by using this method of payment. Your warranty is extended on all purchases as well. Also insurance coverage is automatic when renting a car. As strange as it may sound, the credit card company is your representative and if you didn't get the services you paid for, you can dispute it.

"He who has the money is in control."

All credit card companies offer the same protection clause to their cardholders. "If for any reason you are dissatisfied with services or products rendered, you can dispute payment of these items." In other words, you can instruct your credit card company to stop payment because YOU DIDN'T GET WHAT YOU PAID FOR!!!

Remember these words....."I didn't get what I paid for!" Just keep saying that over and over. The repair facility agreed to be a receiver of credit cards and they are legally held to the credit card companies' business contract.

The repair facility will be charged back in this type of transaction if disputes arise. They will have fifteen to twenty days to provide documentation of the transaction and defend their position in the matter. In most cases they will fail to meet time requirements and the dispute will end there.

If by chance the repair facility does meet the criteria to dispute your claim then the credit card company will attempt to become the mediator in the dispute. Remember, they represent you! Ultimately this payment method is the best ways to take control of a dire situation, ie; withhold funds until you are satisfied. The best part is you can dispute matters up to six months, sometimes even longer. Don't be afraid to demand the "**Service"** you deserve.

Ultimately if no agreement is reached you get the money back. Then the other party has to pursue collecting money from you in small claims court.... costing them money, not you.

If they pursue litigation then countersue. Most people don't realize that they can be sued for suing, if a claim is deemed frivolous. Many times the issue gets dropped there. Then ask for a judgment and watch everything change.

I recently went to my bank, and chatted to a few of the tellers who gave me blank stares when asked about how this particular method of retaliation worked, if applied as a debit card. They really didn't know....*Wow!* So I tried it. I purchased a couple of online subscriptions and stopped payment after a couple months, stating "I didn't get what I paid for."

I got all my money back and never heard anything further. Could it be that easy? I have helped numerous people get back thousands of dollars in just this manner.

Finding an honest repair facility in today's world is possible if you remember these tips; Ask around, look at repair facility's rating on www.yelp.com and other ratings apps. Call your AAA representative or 1-800 Let Napa for an A+ rated repair. It won't be the cheapest option but it is the best the industry has to offer. Also many Napa Auto Care Centers are AAA approved facilities. Any repair performed at either one of these types of facilities is warranted for twelve months or twelve-thousand miles.

Tip: Towing insurance makes sense. Use it once a year and it will pay for itself! AAA will tow your car all the way to your auto repair guy especially if you have an exotic car because you don't want just anyone repairing it, if you break down.

I once had a customer who had his classic car towed for free by AAA and brought it to me when it had problems at a car show in Las Vegas. Gave the customer a ride also.

Remember, when you call a perspective repair facility; are they listening to the description of your problem? Are they willing to take a test drive with you, if needed? Did they write up a service order properly, and agreed to give you your old parts back?

If something doesn't turn out as expected, are they willing to continue working on your car, without charging you an arm and a leg?

Most of all, remember to pay with a credit card so you're in control of the final outcome.

Make truth and justice the "American" way again! Make fair prices and an honest day's labor part of your expectations and get what you paid for!

Recently Ripped Off?

How many times have you been ripped off within the last six months, and paid with a credit card? Go get your money back! Right now! Do it!

It really is that simple. Just ten minutes on the phone. The phone number can be found on your billing statement. Call the number on the back of your card.

Remember the old adage "You get what you pay for?" Well, and then think about it this way; you won't get what you didn't pay for. Should you pay for protection? Heck yeah! This is your investment we're talking about.

Buy **AAA** and have a peace of mind. Free jump starts, emergency roadside service for pennies a day, and they even bring you gas. AAA offers travel benefits and discounts nationwide on an array of services, with membership.. They will even handle DMV transactions for you!

Worth saying again: call once year and the service pays for itself. This is called a "no brainer."

Tips For the Road

Have you considered renting a car for a long vacation instead of driving the family car? If problems occur on the trip remember, your own car is still in your driveway at home safe and sound.

Been thinking of buying a new car? Rent one first to see if you really like it. When rental agencies try to charge you for extra insurance, remember most credit cards will cover that expense. The protection offered by your credit card company is the same in all types of transactions, not just Cars!

Didn't get what you paid for? Take the money back. Don't be afraid to demand quality products and solid customer service.

Car Tips

- Get gas when it's cool so you will get more volume for your money. Don't top up your tank. Needs room to expand.

- Pump your fuel slowly so the vapor recovery system at the pump doesn't reclaim the gas you paid for.

- The fuel in the pump hose is paid for. Tip up the hose and drain it.

- Add STP Injector cleaner. Black Bottle. To every third or fourth tank of fuel. Add it more concentrated such as to a half tank and run to near empty. This will clean the fine meshed screens in the injectors of particles of dirt that were too small to capture in the fuel filter.

- Don't run your vehicle constantly below a quarter of a tank as the fuel is required for cooling of the fuel pump located in the tank

- Check your tire pressure regularly because they can drop ten pounds when the weather makes that sudden change in spring and fall

- Synthetic oils are best for your car.

- Castrol's straight 30 wt still contains Zinc for flat tappet cams.

- Change brake fluid every three years. It attracts moisture evident by turning black. Water eventually causes damage to aluminum brake components causing failure. By changing your brake fluid you can eliminate the risk of brake component failure.

- Replace break in fluids in your differentials and gear boxes or they will fail by design. Fluids are often too thin and have poor quality for long term lubrication.

- Rubbing alcohol will clean wiper blades off and make them look like new.

- Try *Pine-Sol* for car wash concentrate. It removes bugs and road tar instantly. It leaves a nice shine when buffed with a towel. a quarter cup per gallon of water just like recommended for general cleaning.

- Add fuel injector cleaner to your fuel tank. The screens in the injectors will trap particles too small to be trapped in your fuel filter. You will notice a change in performance within a block of driving. Guaranteed! **Do it now!**

- When was the last time your fuel filter was changed? Consult your owner's manual but I recommend changing your fuel filter every twenty-thousand miles.

- Add two stroke oil to your fuel for them older engines designed to run on high octane leaded gas. It cools the combustion temperature and lubricates the upper cylinder so no damage occurs.

- Swell them old rubber doors seals to be like new with dot 3 brake fluid. Careful of painted surfaces. Spray with silicone spray after 20 minutes to seal.

- Walk around your car every time you get in it. Checking clearances and any damage that may have occurred while parked. Maybe even a low tire.

Useful links

Consumer Protection Agency

(Office of Attorney General)

http://oag.ca.gov/consumers

Bureau of Auto Repair

http://www.bar.ca.gov/Consumer/Auto_Repair_Guide.html

Better Business Bureau

http://www.bbb.org/

Yelp

http://www.yelp.com

AAA

http://www.aaa.com

STP Injector Cleaner

http://www.stp.com/products/fuel-additives/super-concentrated-fuel-injector-cleaner/

What others say about the Author

- **Al Collingbourne, Collingbourne Chevrolet Detroit Michigan**
Gordon Kaesemeyer is the best mechanic on the west coast.

- **Jacqueline K. Pendergrass** Back in 1993 I started working for Gordon at The Shop in Escondido CA. I started as the secretary and over time was promoted to the Office/Service Manager. During this time Gordon taught me all that I knew about auto repair. He knows all aspects of auto repair. He was the owner of a 12 bay Shop Gordon did all types of repairs, from diagnostics of drivability problems, electrical problems, to major repairs. Quite honestly my ultimate job was when I worked for Gordon. It was a learning experience each and every day.
From his teachings, I still to this day am able to take my own vehicles to a repair shop
and be fully aware of an honest or dishonest mechanic. I am also able to help others
when they feel scammed. Gordon is a wealth of knowledge in the field of automotive.

- **Angelo Finocchiaro Jr.** I had one of your original booklets 20 years ago, and helped me to navigate the greedy snakes out there.

- **Mary Baptist** There is no one that knows more about cars than Gordon... He is the Master.. Still call him today. After 25 years. THE BEST

- **Erron Archuleta** "for the last 25 Years I can always call Gordon. I describe what my car is doing or not doing & he can tell me what's wrong with it. "Mr. Diagnostic" for sure. Nobody knows cars more than I call Gordon "The Car Whisperer this man.

Dale Curtis, Baker County Tournements

Gordon Kaesemeyer has been a friend for many years..I knew him in high school and became even better friends when he was mayor of Halfway Oregon. When he was mayor he also had an auto repair shop that was a thriving, business...he helped me out a lot on questions but he also had the dignity and character to help people and treat them honest in his repair shop....dignity, honesty, and character towards people has always been a very top priority to him. Love this guy for he is a great person

Randy Malan *BUBBA* I found the information contained in this book to be well written, easily understood, and practical. *I've* saved thousands of dollars using this information. I'm certain you can too.

www.ingramcontent.com/pod-product-compliance
Lightning Source LLC
Chambersburg PA
CBHW041145180526
45159CB00002BB/733

* 9 7 8 1 5 1 1 4 9 0 3 3 7 *